Shape Hunters

Shapes at School

by Jenny Fretland VanVoorst

Bullfrog
Books

Ideas for Parents and Teachers

Bullfrog Books let children practice reading informational text at the earliest reading levels. Repetition, familiar words, and photo labels support early readers.

Before Reading

- Discuss the cover photo. What does it tell them?

- Look at the picture glossary together. Read and discuss the words.

Read the Book

- "Walk" through the book and look at the photos. Let the child ask questions. Point out the photo labels.

- Read the book to the child, or have him or her read independently.

After Reading

- Prompt the child to think more. Ask: What shapes have you seen in your classroom? On the playground?

Bullfrog Books are published by Jump!
5357 Penn Avenue South
Minneapolis, MN 55419
www.jumplibrary.com

Library of Congress Cataloging-in-Publication Data

Fretland VanVoorst, Jenny, 1972– author.
 Shapes at school / by Jenny Fretland VanVoorst.
   pages cm.—(Shape hunters)
 "Bullfrog Books are published by Jump!."
 Summary: "Carefully leveled text and beautiful full-color photographs take beginning readers on a tour of a typical school environment and encourages them to recognize shapes they see every day." —Provided by publisher.
 Audience: Ages 5–8.
 Audience: Grades K to 3.
 Includes index.
 ISBN 978-1-62031-203-2 (hardcover: alk. paper) —
 ISBN 978-1-62031-253-7 (paperback) —
 ISBN 978-1-62496-290-5 (ebook)
 1. Shapes—Juvenile literature.
 2. Schools—Juvenile literature. I. Title.
 QA445.5.F744 2016
 516.15—dc23
                                    014046837

Series Designer: Ellen Huber
Book Designer: Lindaanne Donohoe

Photo Credits: All photos by Shutterstock except: age fotostock, 22br; Dreamstime, 4, 5; Fotosearch, 16–17; iStock, 6–7, 20, 23tr; SuperStock, 12, 14, 22tr; Thinkstock, 20–21, 22tl.

Printed in the United States of America at Corporate Graphics in North Mankato, Minnesota.

Table of Contents

School Shapes

A school is full
of shapes.

How many can you find?

$$27 + 13 = 40$$
$$45 - 21 = 24$$
$$72 \div 9 = 8$$
$$8 \times 4 = 32$$

Mrs. Paz writes on the chalkboard.

It is a rectangle.

So are our easels.

And the paper.

Let's paint!

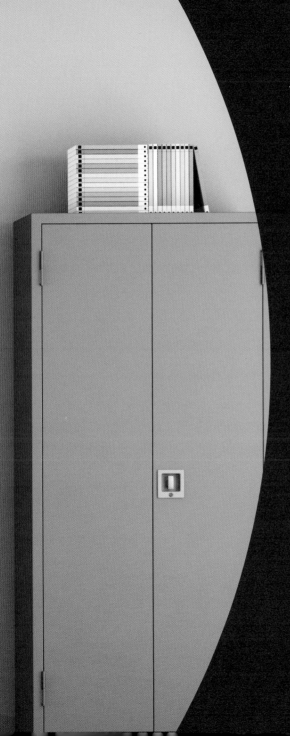

A circle hangs
on the wall.

The clock!

What time is it?

Time for lunch!
Sam takes a tray.

It has rectangles and circles.
They show where the food goes.

Kia brings her lunch.
What will she eat?
A sandwich cut
into triangles.
Yum!

Let's play outside.

This game is
made of squares.

17

This hoop is a circle.

Jed shoots.
Swish!

19

Back to class.

Mr. Oz grades our tests.

What shape is this?

What does it mean?

well done!

More Shapes at School

hearts

squares

rectangle

stars

Picture Glossary

chalkboard
A rectangular board teachers write on to share information with the entire class.

grade
To review work and give it a score.

easel
A frame to hold up an artist's painting.

tray
A large flat plate, often with handles, for carrying items.

Index

To Learn More

Learning more is as easy as 1, 2, 3.

1) Go to www.factsurfer.com

2) Enter "shapesatschool" into the search box.

3) Click the "Surf" button to see a list of websites.

With factsurfer.com, finding more information is just a click away.